BASEBALL LEGENDS

Hank Aaron
Grover Cleveland Alexander
Ernie Banks
Johnny Bench
Yogi Berra
Roy Campanella
Roberto Clemente
Ty Cobb
Dizzy Dean
Joe DiMaggio
Bob Feller
Jimmie Foxx
Lou Gehrig
Bob Gibson
Rogers Hornsby
Reggie Jackson
Shoeless Joe Jackson
Walter Johnson
Sandy Koufax
Mickey Mantle
Christy Mathewson
Willie Mays
Stan Musial
Satchel Paige
Brooks Robinson
Frank Robinson
Jackie Robinson
Pete Rose
Babe Ruth
Nolan Ryan
Mike Schmidt
Tom Seaver
Duke Snider
Warren Spahn
Willie Stargell
Casey Stengel
Honus Wagner
Ted Williams
Carl Yastrzemski
Cy Young

NEWFIELD
PUBLICATIONS

WILLIE MAYS

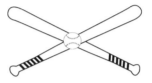

John Grabowski

Introduction by
Jim Murray

Senior Consultant
Earl Weaver

CHELSEA HOUSE PUBLISHERS
New York • Philadelphia

Published by arrangement with
Chelsea House Publishers.
Newfield Publications is a federally
registered trademark of Newfield
Publications, Inc.

Produced by James Charlton Associates
New York, New York.

Designed by Hudson Studio
Ossining, New York.

Typesetting by LinoGraphics
New York, New York.

Picture research by Jennie McGregor
Cover illustration by Dan O'Leary

Library of Congress Cataloging-in-Publication Data

Grabowski, John.
    Willie Mays/John Grabowski.
        p. cm.—(Baseball legends)
    Includes bibliographical references.
    Summary: A biography of the professional baseball player who
played in every All-Star Game from 1954 to 1973.
        ISBN 0-7910-1183-6
        ISBN 0-7910-1217-4 (pbk.)
        1. Mays, Willie. 1931 –   —Juvenile literature. 2. Baseball
players—United States—Biography—Juvenile literature. [1. Mays,
-Biography.] I. Title. II. Series.
GV865.M38G73   1990   89-48947
796.357'092--dc20   CIP
[B]   AC

CONTENTS

WHAT MAKES A STAR 6
Jim Murray

CHAPTER 1
A PREVIEW OF THINGS TO COME 9

CHAPTER 2
EDUCATION OF A BALLPLAYER 13

CHAPTER 3
THE MIRACLE OF COOGAN'S BLUFF 19

CHAPTER 4
NEW YORK HERO 25

CHAPTER 5
GOOD-BYE NEW YORK 31

CHAPTER 6
A FLAG FOR SAN FRANCISCO 39

CHAPTER 7
RECORDS AND HONORS 45

CHAPTER 8
BACK TO WHERE IT ALL BEGAN 51

CHAPTER 9
AMONG THE IMMORTALS 55

CHRONOLOGY 59

STATISTICS 61

FURTHER READING 62

INDEX 63

WHAT MAKES A STAR

Jim Murray

No one has ever been able to explain to me the mysterious alchemy that makes one man a .350 hitter and another player, more or less identical in physical makeup, hard put to hit .200. You look at an Al Kaline, who played with the Detroit Tigers from 1953 to 1974. He was pale, stringy, almost poetic-looking. He always seemed to be struggling against a bad case of mononucleosis. But with a bat in his hands, he was King Kong. During his career, he hit 399 home runs, rapped out 3,007 hits, and compiled a .297 batting average.

Form isn't the reason. The first time anybody saw Roberto Clemente step into the batter's box for the Pittsburgh Pirates, the best guess was that Clemente would be back in Double A ball in a week. He had one foot in the bucket and held his bat at an awkward angle—he looked as though he couldn't hit an outside pitch. A lot of other ballplayers may have had a better-looking stance. Yet they never led the National League in hitting in four different years, the way Clemente did.

Not every ballplayer is born with the ability to hit a curveball. Nor is exceptional hand-eye coordination the key to heavy hitting. Big-league locker rooms are filled with players who have all the attributes, save one: discipline. Every baseball man can tell you a story about a pitcher who throws a ball faster than anyone has ever seen but who has no control on or *off* the field.

The Hall of Fame is full of people who transformed themselves into great ballplayers by working at the sport, by studying the game, and making sacrifices. They're overachievers—and winners. If you want to find them, just watch the World Series. Or simply read about New York Yankee great Lou Gehrig; Ted Williams, "the Splendid Splinter" of the Boston Red Sox; or the Dodgers' strikeout king Sandy Koufax.

A pitcher *should* be able to win a lot of ballgames with a 98-miles-per-hour fastball. But what about the pitcher who wins 20 games a year with a fastball so slow that you can catch it with your teeth? Bob Feller of the Cleveland Indians got into the Hall of Fame with a blazing fastball that glowed in the dark. National League star Grover Cleveland Alexander got there with a pitch that took considerably longer to reach the plate; but when it did arrive, the pitch was exactly where Alexander wanted it to be—and the last place the batter expected it to be.

There are probably more players with exceptional ability who didn't make it to the major leagues than there are who did. A number of great hitters, bored with fielding practice, had to be dropped from their team because their home-run production didn't make up for their lapses in the field. And then there are players like Brooks Robinson of the Baltimore Orioles, who made himself into a human vacuum cleaner at third base because he knew that working hard to become an expert fielder would win him a job in the big leagues.

A star is not something that flashes through the sky. That's a comet. Or a meteor. A star is something you can steer ships by. It stays in place and gives off a steady glow; it is fixed, permanent. A star works at being a star.

And that's how you tell a star in baseball. He shows up night after night and takes pride in how brightly he shines. He's Willie Mays running so hard his hat keeps falling off; Ty Cobb sliding to stretch a single into a double; Lou Gehrig, after being fooled in his first two at-bats, belting the next pitch off the light tower because he's taken the time to study the pitcher. Stars never take themselves for granted. That's why they're stars.

1

A PREVIEW OF THINGS TO COME

After finishing the 1950 baseball season in third place, just five games behind the pennant-winning Philadelphia Phillies, the New York Giants had high hopes for 1951. But little more than a month into the new season, the club was already mired in fifth place with a 17-19 record.

On May 25, however, things began looking up. On that day, a much-heralded rookie joined the Giants, promoted from the minors where he'd been hitting an incredible .477.

Leo Durocher, the Giants' feisty manager, immediately put the nervous youngster into the lineup as the club began a three-game series against the defending-champion Phillies in Philadelphia.

In his first game as a Giant, Willie Mays went 0 for 5 at the plate and misplayed a ball in center field. However, the New Yorkers won the contest. The next two days brought more of the same: Mays remained hitless, but the Giants racked up two more victories.

Mays in New York's Polo Grounds during 1951, his rookie year.

Then the Giants returned to the Polo Grounds, their home field, to play the Boston Braves. His first look at his new stadium must have made the 20-year-old Mays even more nervous. The left- and right-field fences were so close you could almost reach out and touch them from the dugout, but center field was another matter altogether. At 483 feet, the distance from home plate to straightaway center was the farthest in the major leagues. Mays's splendid speed and cannon-like throwing arm would be sorely tested with so much acreage to cover.

In his first appearance before the hometown

Mays slides head first into third base against the Cardinals.

fans, Mays came up against Boston's ace pitcher, Warren Spahn. In the bottom of the first, Spahn retired the first two Giant batters. And then it was Mays's turn.

Looking for an easy third out, Spahn decided to start the newcomer off with a fastball. It was his first mistake of the night. Mays took a mighty swing and blasted the ball over the left-field roof!

As he rounded the bases, young Willie Mays had no way of knowing that he would travel the same pathway 659 more times before retiring years later. All he knew then was that he finally had got his first big-league hit.

2

EDUCATION OF A BALLPLAYER

After batting .477 for the American Association's Minneapolis Millers, Mays was called up to the New York Giants in 1951.

Willie Howard Mays was born in the small town of Westfield, Alabama, on May 6, 1931. His parents—William Howard Mays and Ann Sattlewhite—separated when he was just 3 years old. Willie was brought up by his father, a railroad porter, and two orphaned neighborhood girls who moved in to help raise the child. Though neither was much older than Willie, "Aunt" Sarah and "Aunt" Ernestine earned his love and affection.

When Willie was 10 years old, his father got a job in the steel mills closer to home. Willie attended Fairfield High School, where he was a triple threat at baseball, football, and basketball.

"I knew Willie was good about the time he was fourteen," his father would later recall. "He played on the mill team against grown men, and it was easy to see that he could out-hit and out-run them."

While still in high school, Willie caught the eye of Piper Davis, manager of the Negro American League Birmingham Black Barons. Until

The main street of Fairfield, Alabama in 1945, where Willie Mays went to high school.

1946, when Branch Rickey signed a young black player named Jackie Robinson to a contract with the Brooklyn Dodgers, the Negro Leagues provided the only opportunity for black ballplayers to showcase their talents before an audience. Davis recognized Mays's tremendous natural abilities and offered him $250 a month to play for the Barons. He became a second father to young Willie, teaching him the intricacies and fine points of the game.

By playing with the Barons, young "Buck," as Willie was called then, was no longer eligible to compete in sports for his high school teams. But the Fairfield principal, E. T. Oliver, was more concerned with Willie's academic career. He feared that ball practice would cut into class time. Mays vowed that would not happen. And he kept his word, continuing his education and receiving his high school diploma.

The Barons played their home games at old Rickwood Field in Birmingham. In his two seasons with the team (1948 and 1949), Mays did it all, displaying a powerful arm and exceptional running speed, swinging an explosive bat, and performing acrobatic fielding magic. The fans came out to cheer the Barons and their star, who was also the youngest player on the club.

Perhaps the highlight of Mays's two seasons with Birmingham was his appearance in the 1948 Negro League World Series against the legendary Homestead Grays. Little did he know that in three short years he'd be playing in another World Series, this time as a Giant against the legendary New York Yankees.

Were it not for a twist of fate, Willie Mays might have signed his first professional contract with the Brooklyn Dodgers or Boston Braves instead of the New York Giants. New York scout Eddie Montague had been given a lead on a young Baron first baseman, Alonzo Perry, whom the Giants were considering for their Sioux City farm team. But when Montague showed up to see Perry, he was overwhelmed by the young centerfielder Mays. Upon learning that Mays had never signed a formal contract with Birmingham, Montague quickly signed him up for a $4,000 bonus and a salary of $250 per month. Willie was assigned to Sioux City in Class A ball, but never played there. A racial incident several days earlier had created tension in the town, and the farm club was afraid there'd be more trouble if a black joined the team.

So instead of starting his pro career in Class A, Mays was assigned to the lower Class B Interstate League, where he joined the Trenton team in Hagerstown, Maryland. His new manager, Chick Genovese, immediately slipped Mays into the starting lineup in center field. Almost from the start, Mays began to wish he were somewhere else!

Although Mays did not get a single hit in the

SUCH A ONE IS

A-MAYS-ING!

Willie

A caricature of Willie Mays that appeared in the Minneapolis Tribune *when Willie was called up to the major leagues.*

four-game series against the Braves' farm club, that was not the worst of it. Even harder for him to accept was the fact that he could not stay in the same hotel as the rest of his teammates. Hagerstown was segregated, and Mays was the first black ever to play in the Interstate League. He was forced to stay in a small hotel for blacks.

Manager Genovese understood the pressures facing his young star and took a special interest in him. He spent as much time as he could with the lonely rookie, even joining him for meals in the kitchens of segregated restaurants.

Genovese also knew talent when he saw it. He stuck with Mays, who soon began hitting with a vengeance and finished the season with a batting average of .353 for 81 games. His power was not yet fully developed, however. The muscular 5–foot–10, 170-pound frame that would eventually propel 660 balls over major league fences managed only 4 home runs and 55 RBI's in 1950.

Impressed with Mays's showing, the Giants sent him to their Minneapolis club in the AAA American Association for 1951.

Mays got off to a great start with the Minneapolis Millers. He had an excellent spring training under manager Tommy Heath, and his hot hitting continued into the regular season. In just over a month, his batting average skyrocketed to .477. Over the course of one home stand at Nicollet Park in Minneapolis, he got 38 hits in 63 at-bats for an incredible .608 average.

Word of Mays's heroics quickly spread to the major-league front office back in New York. In just 35 games he'd already collected 18 doubles, 3 triples, 8 home runs, and 30 RBI's. So it was no surprise to the Minneapolis fans when he was called up to the parent club late that May.

What was surprising was an advertisement that ran in the *Minneapolis Tribune* on May 27th. Giants owner Horace Stoneham took out an ad to apologize to the fans and explain why their star was being taken away from them. It read, in part, as follows:

"We feel that the Minneapolis fans, who have so enthusiastically supported the Minneapolis club, are entitled to an explanation for the player deal that on Friday transferred outfielder Willie Mays from the Millers to the New York Giants. We appreciate his worth to the Millers, but in all fairness, Mays himself must be a factor in these considerations. Merit must be recognized. On the record of his performance since the American Association season started, Mays is entitled to his promotion, and the chance to prove that he can play major league baseball. It would be most unfair to deprive him of the opportunity he earned with his play."

And so Willie Mays set off for the big leagues.

3

THE MIRACLE OF COOGAN'S BLUFF

Despite Mays's home run against Spahn in his fourth game as a Giant, his struggles to hit major league pitching were not yet over. The next four games saw him go hitless, giving him a .040 batting average in his first 25 at-bats.

After one of those games, Giants manager Leo Durocher found Mays crying in front of his locker. Durocher put his arm around the rookie's shoulders and asked him what was wrong. When Mays spilled out that he might never be able to hit big-league pitching, Durocher reassured him. "As long as I'm manager of the Giants," he said, "you're my centerfielder. You're the greatest ballplayer I ever saw or ever hope to see."

That show of confidence apparently did the trick. Mays proceeded to hit .375 over the next week, and the Giants began to win consistently.

As the team's record improved, Mays became a favorite with the New York fans. They especially appreciated his obvious love for the game and the way he seemed to give it his all. The sight of Mays's hat flying off his head as he raced after

From the start, Giants' manager Leo Durocher was one of Mays' biggest boosters.

fly balls and dashed around the bases became a familiar sight and always raised a cheer. (Only years later did Mays confess to losing his hat on purpose—he always wore one that was a size too large!)

It seemed that Mays couldn't get enough of baseball. Following day games at the Polo Grounds, he would return to the home of David and Anna Goosby, the couple with whom he was staying. He could usually be found outside playing stickball in the streets of Harlem with the neighborhood kids, a practice that made him even more popular.

During the day, Mays would watch and learn from the team's veteran players, men like second baseman Eddie Stanky and outfielder Monte Irvin (Mays's roommate and fellow Negro League star). Feeling more and more comfortable with each passing day, the young star sparked the Giants as they attempted to narrow the distance between themselves and their archrivals, the Brooklyn Dodgers.

By August 11th, however, even Mays was

A favorite with New York fans, Mays was often seen playing stickball with neighborhood children in the streets of Harlem.

getting discouraged. The Giants trailed the Dodg-ers by 13½ games with only 44 left on their schedule. But what happened from that date on has become part of baseball legend — the great-est stretch run by any team in the history of baseball.

The Dodgers continued to play well, winning 26 of their last 49 games for a .531 pace. But that wasn't good enough against the suddenly near-perfect Giants. They won 37 of their final 44 contests, including a streak of 16 in a row, and finished the season in a flat-footed tie with the Brooklyn "Bums." The Giants' run was so amazing that it became forever known as "The Miracle of Coogan's Bluff." (Coogan's Bluff was the New York area where the Polo Grounds was located.)

To break the tie, a best-of-three-game playoff was scheduled. The opening game would be played at the Dodgers' home, Ebbets Field, in Brooklyn.

The entire city was in a frenzy as the two teams faced off that October 1st afternoon. The visitors drew first blood, defeating the Dodgers 3–1 behind the pitching of 17 game winner Jim Hearn. Bobby Thomson and Monte Irvin sup-plied the power by hitting home runs.

The next day Brooklyn evened the series at one game apiece when a rookie pitcher named Clem Labine shut out the Giants 10–0.

And so, after 156 games, the entire season would now come down to one contest. The team that won game 3 would go on to face the mighty New York Yankees in an all–New York World Series.

The Dodgers jumped out to an early lead and were ahead 4–1 going into the bottom of the 9th inning. Dodger hurler Don Newcombe then gave

Mays' rookie season ended dramatically when Bobby Thomson hit "The Shot Heard 'Round the World" to give New York the pennant. Mays (third from right) greets Thomson at home plate.

up three hits to the first four Giants he faced, and then the score was 4–2. With the tying run on second, Ralph Branca came in to relieve the obviously tiring Newcombe.

As Bobby Thomson came to the plate, Mays nervously moved into the on-deck position. Unless Thomson got on base, the Giants' last hope would ride on the broad shoulders of the suddenly insecure youngster. He had gone 1 for 10 thus far in the three games, striking out three times. As Mays would later recall, he was crouched in the on-deck circle praying, "Please don't let it be me. Don't make me come to bat now, God."

Mays never did reach the batter's box. Thomson whacked Branca's second pitch into the left-field seats for a game-winning three-run homer. The most famous hit in baseball history, known as "The Shot Heard 'Round the World," blasted the Giants and their star rookie right into the World Series.

The Series proved to be a letdown, however. Although the Giants won two of the first three games, they couldn't keep it up. Physically and emotionally drained from their incredible pennant run, the Giants were no match for the well-rested Yankees. The "Bronx Bombers" took the next three games in a row to win the championship.

Mays capped off his rookie season with a disappointing Series performance—only 4 hits in 22 at-bats for a .182 average. Moreover, all his hits were singles, and he drove in just one lone run. But his regular season performance was good enough to make him the National League's Rookie of the Year. He earned the award by pounding out 22 doubles, 5 triples, and 20 home runs while hitting for a .274 average. With his base running skills and fielding prowess added in, it was no wonder manager Durocher thought Mays was great. "If he could cook," Durocher raved, "I'd marry him."

4

NEW YORK HERO

When Mays returned to Alabama after the Series, he found a letter from the Selective Service Board waiting for him. The Korean War was still going on then, and he was told to report to his local draft board. After passing his physical and aptitude tests, he knew it was only a matter of time until he would be called upon to serve his country.

Mays joined the Giants at spring training the next year in preparation for the '52 season. It was a difficult time for him because he knew he wouldn't be around long enough to contribute much to his teammates' efforts to defend their National League title.

Despite a slow start by their young star, the Giants started the season strong. By the time Mays left for Fort Eustis at the end of May, they were in first place. But they cooled off without him and eventually finished second behind the Dodgers.

Although his ballplaying was confined to service games for the rest of 1952 and all of 1953, Mays still managed to fine-tune his re-

The Giants' high hopes for a successful defense of their 1951 pennant plummeted when Mays was inducted into the army in May 1952.

markable skills. It was then that he perfected the "basket" catch that would be his trademark for years to come. Rather than catch fly balls with his arms extended over his head, as most players did, Mays began catching them with his glove pocket face-up, directly in front of his stomach. This unorthodox move allowed him to get his hands in position to release his throw just a fraction of a second faster—a small, but definite, advantage.

Throughout his tour of duty at Fort Eustis, Mays stayed in touch with the Giants' manager. Durocher kept after him like a mother hen, always looking ahead to the day Mays would return to civilian life.

That day finally arrived—March 1, 1954. Mays joined the Giants at their spring training camp in Phoenix, Arizona, and the mood in camp began to perk up immediately. Without their star outfielder, the Giants had fallen on hard times, finishing the 1953 season 35 games behind the Dodgers. With him, however, it was a whole other story.

The Giants opened the 1954 campaign against Brooklyn, a game Mays won with a home run. And that was just the beginning. Mays kept belting out homers at a record pace, and by the time the All-Star break came around in July, the Giants were 5½ games in front of the Dodgers.

The All-Star Game had special meaning for Mays, as it was the first of a record 24 in which he would appear. As Ted Williams later put it, "They invented the All-Star Game for him."

Shortly after the All-Star Game, Mays's Aunt Sarah, his "second mother," died. His real mother had passed away less than a year earlier while Mays was still in the Army. Though both trage- dies touched him deeply, Mays did not let them affect his play. Mays's hot hitting continued for the rest of the season. His home-run production dropped off, however, when Durocher asked him to concentrate on getting base hits rather than going for the fences.

The Giants held on to first place, clinching the pennant in the last week of the season. Mays capped his first full season in the majors by winning the National League's batting title with a .345 average. His 13 triples and .667 slugging percentage were also tops in the National League. His final stats included 41 home runs, 110 RBI's, 119 runs scored, and 8 stolen bases.

Following the end of the regular season, the city of New York honored its heroes with a parade down Broadway to City Hall. But even as the players listened to the cheering crowds, they knew their job was not yet complete. They still had to face the challenge of playing "the best team in baseball"—the Cleveland Indians—in the World Series.

The Indians had earned that title by winning 111 games, an American League record, and finishing 8 games ahead of the Yankees. Their lineup featured the A.L. home-run and RBI champ Larry Doby, All-Star third baseman Al Rosen, and batting champion Bobby Avila.

But the real strength of this Cleveland team was its exceptional pitching staff. The starters included three future Hall of Famers, Bob Lemon (23–7), Early Wynn (23–11), and Bob Feller (13–3). And Mike Garcia, another starter, had 19 wins and the lowest earned run average in the league.

Cleveland was the overwhelming favorite as the Series got underway at the Polo Grounds on September 29th. Lemon would start for the Indians, while the Giants sent veteran Sal Maglie to the mound.

The Giants managed to stay even for seven innings, and the score was 2–2 in the top of the 8th. But then the Indians rallied. Their first two hitters got on base, bringing first baseman Vic Wertz to bat. The left-handed slugger had gotten three straight hits off Maglie, so manager Durocher went to his bullpen and brought out southpaw Don Liddle. Wertz swung at Liddle's first pitch and hit a tremendous drive to straightaway center field, surely good for extra bases.

Mays turned and ran full speed toward the distant bleachers, the number 24 on his uniform diminishing in the distance. As he neared the wall, he glanced over his shoulder, caught sight of the ball, and caught it with his back to home plate some 440 feet away. In one fluid motion, he wheeled around and hurled the ball back to the infield. Larry Doby, who had been on second base, tagged up and went to third, but no runs scored.

The entire sequence of events happened so

After tracking down Vic Wertz' drive some 440 feet from home plate in Game 1 of the 1954 World Series, Mays made "The Catch" and baseball history.

fast, it took a moment for the fans to realize what they had seen. A sure-thing bases-clearing hit had been turned into a long out by what may well have been the greatest catch in World Series history.

The Giants got out of the inning without allowing a run, and the game remained tied through the 9th inning.

In the bottom of the 10th, Mays walked and then stole second. After third baseman Hank Thompson was intentionally passed, Durocher sent pinch-hitter Dusty Rhodes, a lefty, up to bat for Irvin.

Rhodes drove Lemon's first pitch toward the right-field foul pole. The ball just made it into the stands in fair territory some 270 feet away, and the three-run homer gave the Giants an opening game victory.

In game 2, New York's 21-game winner, Johnny Antonelli, faced Early Wynn and the Indians. The 25-year-old lefty went all the way for the Giants, with a 3–1 victory.

The Series moved to Cleveland's Municipal Stadium for games 3 and 4, but it made no difference to the high-flying Giants. They won the final two games by 6–2 and 7–4 counts to sweep the Indians and become world champions.

In addition to his fabulous fielding, Mays contributed to the Series sweep with 4 hits in 14 at-bats (.286), 3 RBI's and 4 runs scored. And his dream season ended on the highest note possible when he was named the National League's Most Valuable Player.

5

GOOD–BYE NEW YORK

Although the Giants were world champions, the feeling in training camp the next spring was surprisingly subdued. Giants owner Horace Stoneham and manager Durocher were rumored to be feuding, and many people thought that Durocher might soon be leaving the team.

The Giants started off slowly in 1955, with several on the injury list. Then, toward the end of the season, Durocher confirmed the rumors—he would not be returning as manager in 1956.

Mays was stunned. He'd come to rely on Durocher as a constant source of encouragement. Where would he go and who would he turn to if he needed help and Durocher wasn't there?

But Durocher wasn't gone yet. And, as always, he knew just what to say. "Willie Mays doesn't need help from anyone," he declared.

Durocher was right. Although the Giants wound up in third place, 18½ games behind Brooklyn, Mays finished in fine form. He slugged a league-leading 51 home runs to tie the Giants' all-time single-season mark set by Johnny Mize back in 1947. He also topped the league in

Following the Giants' final game at the Polo Grounds in 1957—a 9-1 loss to the Pirates—Mays lingers to give his New York fans something to remember him by.

31

triples (13) and slugging percentage (.659) and was second in batting average (.319), RBI's (127), runs scored (123), and stolen bases (24). His fielding was just as impressive. He led all N.L. outfielders with 23 assists.

Mays may have lost the most important person in his professional life, but before the next season began he would gain one in his personal life—a wife! On Valentine's Day he married Marghuerite Wendell. The newlyweds moved into a home in upper Manhattan shortly before Mays left for spring training.

Bill Rigney, a former teammate of Mays in 1951, had been hired to replace Durocher. He greeted the club and new media with talk of a new beginning; but once the season started, it was the same old story. The Giants quickly dropped into the second division, and attendance figures dropped, too, as the fans lost faith in their team.

With many of his old teammates gone to other teams by way of trades, the young Mays suddenly found himself a "veteran." He did his best to take on a leadership role, but he missed his own leader—Leo Durocher. Mays managed to have a good year anyway, leading the league in stolen bases with 40. But when the team finished a dismal sixth in the standings, rumors circulated that the club might consider leaving New York and relocating elsewhere.

The 1957 season was a replay of 1956, with the Giants again winding up sixth, and attendance figures lower than ever. The team announced it would be moving to San Francisco in '58—accompanying the Dodgers, who were making the move from Brooklyn to Los Angeles.

The final game at the Polo Grounds symbolized the frustrations of the entire season as the

Giants lost 9–1 to the last-place Pittsburgh Pirates. And with that, seventy-five years of National League baseball in New York came to an end. Intent on letting the Giants' management know how they felt about it, the fans in attendance streamed out onto the field and proceeded to dismantle the park. Anything and everything that could be taken, was—including bases, signs, and patches of turf.

Of course, what the New Yorkers really wanted was to keep was their number-one star. They weren't the only ones who wanted Mays. General Manager Frank Lane of the St. Louis Cardinals had offered the Giants $1 million for Mays, an incredible amount in the 1950's. But with his awesome physical talents plus his unbridled joy and enthusiasm for the game, Mays was worth even more to his fans. And now the Giants were taking him 3,000 miles away.

Mays once said, "When I was 17 years old, I realized I was in a form of show business.... So I played for the fans, and I wanted to make sure each fan that came out would see something

Mays, Alvin Dark, Monte Irvin, and Bobby Hofman (left to right) were part of the World Championship Giants team in 1954.

different I did each day."

Mays had certainly given them something to see. In his final year as a New York Giant, he batted .333, with 35 homers, 97 RBI's, 112 runs scored, while leading the league in slugging percentage (.626), triples (20), and stolen bases (38). He also became the first player in N.L. history to record 20 or more doubles, triples, homers, and stolen bases in one season.

Strangely enough, the San Francisco fans did not exactly welcome Mays with open arms. Although it had never had its own big-league team before, San Francisco boasted not one but two minor-league franchises, and many native San Franciscans made it to the majors. The greatest of these players was Joe DiMaggio, the Yankees' Hall of Fame centerfielder.

Even before the Giants came to town, manager Rigney tried to stir up interest in the team by building up its star player. Somehow, this strategy seemed to backfire. San Franciscans appeared to almost resent Mays.

Mays did his best to win them over. Always one to give 100 percent every minute he was on the field, he tried to do even more than usual, taking charge of the young club. The result was a strong start for both Mays and the Giants.

But as the season went on, Mays suddenly found himself feeling extremely tired. Things got so bad that he became convinced he had some serious illness. Mays went so far as to check himself into a New York hospital but was released when the doctors concluded he was suffering only from exhaustion.

The fatigue took its toll, however, and his batting average plummeted. The team's inexperience and lack of pitching depth began to show, and the Giants finished their first West Coast

Mays poses after scoring the 1,000th major league run of his career on September 9, 1961.

season in third place, 12 games behind the Braves.

Mays again led the league in stolen bases (31) and runs scored (121), however, and was second in batting (.347), slugging percentage (.583), hits (208), and triples (11). Giant rookie Orlando Cepeda finished at .312, with the same number of RBI's as Mays (96) and four fewer home runs (25 to 29). However, when readers of the *San Francisco Chronicle* were asked to vote for the team's Most Valuable Player, Cepeda came out on top. The local fans had given further evidence of resentment to the "imported" hero.

The snub may have hurt Mays's feelings, but it didn't hurt his play. He came back with a solid 1959 season, again leading the league in stolen bases, even after playing the last two months of the season with a broken finger. The injury—the first serious one in Mays's career—was kept secret so opposing teams would not use it to their advantage.

Meanwhile, Cepeda defied the "sophomore jinx," increasing his production in nearly every category, and the Giants' fortunes improved. That wasn't enough to win the team a pennant, however. In contention right to the end, the Giants finally folded and finished 4 games behind Los Angeles in third place.

For their first two years in San Francisco, the Giants played in Seals Stadium, which had originally opened back in 1931. But the city had agreed to build a new stadium, Candlestick Park, and that was ready for the beginning of the 1960 season.

Located near San Francisco Bay, Candlestick quickly became known for its cold and windy conditions. Every ball hit into the air became an unknown quantity, with pop-ups carrying out to the fences and easy fly balls falling between fielders. Visiting players hated coming to Candlestick Park.

Nevertheless, the Giants managed to get off to a good start in their new home. But apparently it wasn't good enough to satisfy owner Stoneham. He fired Rigney as manager and hired Tom Sheehan, former head of the scouting department, to take his place. And still the team floundered, despite another solid season from Mays. This time the Giants finished in fifth place, 16 games off the pace.

In 1961, Sheehan was replaced by Alvin Dark, another former Giant player, and the team took on a definite New York look when Dark brought in three new coaches—Larry Jansen, Whitey Lockman, and Wes Westrum—who had all been members of the 1951 pennant-winning Giants.

Mays started slowly and was in a bit of a

slump when the Giants traveled to Milwaukee to play the Braves in late April. Following a win on the 29th, he went out to eat with Willie McCovey, the powerful young first baseman who had joined the Giants in '59. They brought some ribs back to the hotel with them, but the food apparently didn't agree with Mays—he was up most of the night with an upset stomach.

The next day, tired and drained, he left for the ballpark with every intention of not playing. But once he got there, he borrowed a bat from teammate Joey Amalfitano, and decided to give it his best shot. His best shot turned out to be something to behold. Mays had a game mere mortals only dream about. He clouted a record-tying 4 homers and drove in 8 runs, breaking out of his slump in spectacular fashion.

Mays went on to another super season, hitting 40 home runs, scoring a league-leading 129 runs, and driving in 123 runners. But despite his efforts, the Giants had to settle for another third-place finish, 8 games behind the Cincinnati Reds. Still, the atmosphere in the clubhouse had definitely improved. Hopes were running high for the 1962 season.

The starting lineup of the new San Francisco Giants consisted of (left to right): Jim Davenport (3b); Danny O'Connell (2B); Willie Mays (CF); Willie Kirkland (RF); Orlando Cepeda (1B); Hank Sauer (LF); Daryl Spencer (SS); Valmy Thomas (C); and Ruben Gomez (P). In their first game on the West Coast, they defeated the Dodgers 8-0.

6

A FLAG FOR SAN FRANCISCO

Over the years, the Dodger-Giant rivalry had developed into one of the greatest in all of sports. The 1962 season would once again see the two teams battle down to the wire for the National League championship.

The Giants' greatest power was at the plate. In '62, Mays would lead the league with 49 home runs, while driving in a career-high 141 runs. He, Orlando Cepeda, Felipe Alou, Willie McCovey, Tom Haller, and Ed Bailey formed the nucleus of a squad that would lead the National League in runs scored, home runs, and batting average.

Unlike their powerful predecessors in Brooklyn, the L.A. Dodgers built their strength on the mound and on the basepaths (although they did boast the league's batting and RBI champ in Tommy Davis). Don Drysdale, Sandy Koufax, Johnny Podres, and Stan Williams were the starting pitchers. They were backed up by a strong bullpen featuring Ron Perranoski, Larry Sherry, and Ed Roebuck.

The team's point of attack, however, centered on 29-year-old shortstop Maury Wills. In

Two-year-old Michael Mays visits his dad at spring training in 1961.

1962, Wills became the most feared base stealer in the majors, pilfering an incredible 104 bases to nearly triple his previous year's total. And in the process, he broke Ty Cobb's all-time single-season record of 96 steals, set back in 1915.

As the season wound down, things looked bleak for the Giants. The 31-year-old Mays was feeling the effects of the long, hot summer. During an important September game in Cincinnati, he passed out in the Giants' dugout. He was rushed to the hospital, where extreme exhaustion was again diagnosed.

Manager Dark kept Mays out of the lineup for three games. "Nobody . . .wants to win a pennant more than I," he stated. "But I'm not going to do it at the risk of shattering somebody's nerves, perhaps permanently."

Mays came back on September 16th against Pittsburgh and celebrated by slugging his 44th home run of the season. Nevertheless, the Giants lost the game. With just 7 games left to play, the team found itself 4 games behind the first-place Dodgers. Then the Dodgers lost Koufax's ser-

Mays is carried from the dugout on a stretcher after passing out from exhaustion in a 1962 game against Cincinnati.

vices due to an injury, and their lead quickly dwindled. But they managed to hold on and were still ahead by one game as the final day of the season dawned.

In order to tie L.A., the Giants would have to beat Houston and hope that the Dodgers lost to St. Louis. The Giants and Colt 45s, as the Houston club was then named, were tied 1–1 going into the 8th inning. With the whole season on the line, Mays slugged a Dick Farrell fastball for a home run and a 2–1 victory for his team. The Giants had done all they could do. Now it was up to the Cardinals.

Mays and his teammates gathered around a radio in the clubhouse to hear the final moments of the L.A.–St. Louis contest. A solo home run by Cardinals catcher Gene Oliver proved to be the only score of the game, but it was enough to put the Giants and the Dodgers into a tie for first place!

In a replay of their 1951 showdown, the two teams would meet in a best-of-three playoff to determine the pennant winner.

The Giants took the opening game, with left-hander Billy Pierce shutting out the Dodgers. Mays contributed two home runs and a single to the 8–0 victory. The Dodgers, however, bounced back to win the second game, after trailing 5–0 early in the contest.

Just as in 1951, this season would be decided on the basis of one big game. Coincidentally, the game would be played on October 3rd—exactly 11 years after Thomson's legendary home run gave the Giants the 1951 flag.

The Giants scored early in the contest, but the Dodgers fought back to lead 4–2 going into the 9th. Then, with the bases loaded and one out, Mays came to the plate against ace reliever

Mays's catch off the bat of Roger Maris helps the Giants beat the Yankees in game 4 of the 1962 World Series.

Ed Roebuck, and drilled an infield hit off the pitcher's glove. Now the score was 4–3. Before the inning ended, a sacrifice fly, wild pitch, intentional walk, unintentional walk, and error had given the Giants three more runs and a 6–4 lead.

First-game starter Billy Pierce came in to get the final three outs in the bottom half of the 9th, with the last coming on a drive to Mays. After making the catch, Mays hurled the ball into the stands in an emotional outburst of joy.

History had repeated itself. Once again the Giants had won the final game of a playoff against the Dodgers by coming from behind in the last inning. And still again, they would go on to face the New York Yankees in the World Series.

This time, the two teams took turns winning, splitting the first six games. The 7th and deciding game would match two right-handers, the Yankees' Ralph Terry and the Giants' Jack

Sanford.

The New Yorkers scored once in the 5th inning, and that run held up into the 9th. Then, with two outs and Matty Alou on first, it was once more up to Mays. And as usual, Mays came through. He lined a double down the right-field line to put the tying run on third and the go-ahead run on second. But the next man up, Willie McCovey, hit a line drive to second base-man Bobby Richardson for the final out.

Although the Yankees won the world championship, the Giants—and Mays in particular—had won something almost as valuable: for the first time since coming out west, Mays received the hometown fans' cheers and adulation. It had taken five years, but the San Franciscans were finally starting to appreciate Willie Mays.

7

RECORDS AND HONORS

While Willie Mays was winning fans in San Francisco, a new N.L. franchise, the New York Mets, was playing its home games in the old Polo Grounds until a new stadium could be built for them.

New York had never been far from Mays's heart. In fact, Willie, his wife Marghuerite, and their adopted son Michael had returned to make their home there following the 1959 season. Unfortunately, Mays and his wife began to drift apart. By the time the 1963 season started, divorce proceedings were under way, with Mays in San Francisco and Marghuerite and Michael living in New York.

Mays was having financial problems then, too, having made several bad investments. As a result, even though he would be paid $105,000 in 1963—more than any other baseball player— he was nearly bankrupt.

With so much on his mind, it was hardly surprising when Mays got off to the poorest start of his big-league career.

One of the few bright spots early in the

In 1965, Mays receives his second MVP Award after batting .317, hitting 52 home runs, scoring 118 runs, and driving in 112.

season was Willie Mays Night at the Polo Grounds. Nearly 50,000 fans showed up to watch the Giants play the Mets and to honor their favorite son, even though he was now wearing a San Francisco uniform. Their love was evident when Bill Shea, who helped bring National League baseball back to New York, addressed the crowd before the game.

"We want to know," said Shea, "Mr. Stoneham, Horace Stoneham, president of the Giants, when are you going to give us back our Willie Mays?"

The fans went wild, and for the moment at least, all Mays's troubles were forgotten. But then it was back to San Francisco and still one more thing to worry about.

As often happens when a team does not play up to its potential, tension began mounting in the Giants' clubhouse. As the team struggled, several players—including Mays—had run-ins with manager Alvin Dark.

Although Mays perked up after the All-Star break, the club never quite put it all together. The pressure of trying to carry the team on his shoulders took its toll on Mays, who once again was hospitalized for fatigue. He managed to finish out the season, but the Giants could not catch the Dodgers, who went on to win the National League pennant.

In 1964, Mays continued to make his way up the all-time listings in several categories, but the Giants continued to meet with frustration.

Some unfortunate remarks by manager Dark nearly led to a revolt by the black and Latin American players on the team. Mays helped defend Dark against their charges of racism and put down the uprising. "If I go back with Alvin Dark," he said, "it means one thing: I know him better than any of the rest of you. I know when he helped me and I know why."

Shortly thereafter, Mays was named team captain. He did his best to hold the club together, but the damage had already been done. The Giants finished in fourth place, 3 games out of first, despite a league-leading 47 home runs from Mays.

Herman Franks replaced Dark in 1965, and Mays responded with an all-time Giants single-season record of 52 homers, including a National League record of 17 in the month of August. On September 13th, he hit his 500th career home run. The blast put him in fifth place on the all-time list, behind Hall of Famers Babe Ruth (714), Jimmie Foxx (534), Ted Williams (521), and Mel Ott (511). Mays also scored more than 100 runs for the 12th consecutive year, and drove in over 100 for the 7th straight season. His efforts brought him his second Most Valuable Player award.

But Mays's value to his team went way beyond his bat, as a shocking incident late that season clearly showed.

Mays shows the super swing that accounted for 660 home runs, more than any other major leaguer except Henry Aaron and Babe Ruth.

On August 22nd, the Dodgers and Giants met at Candlestick Park for an important game in the hotly contested pennant race. Los Angeles catcher John Roseboro fired a ball back to pitcher Sandy Koufax, just missing the head of the San Francisco batter, pitcher Juan Marichal. Some heated words were exchanged and then Marichal took his bat and clubbed Roseboro over the head three times.

As players erupted from both benches, Mays charged toward the plate and dragged Roseboro away from the fray, cradling the catcher's bleeding head in his arms. His actions helped prevent further injury to a friend who happened to be a member of the opposing team.

Later, in deciding not to suspend Marichal for his actions, National League president Warren Giles took into account the effect the loss of its star pitcher would have on the Giants' pennant chances.

"Shall I penalize Willie Mays?" said Giles. "If so, how does such fine and decent conduct deserve a penalty? This man was an example of the best in any of us."

Although the Giants finished the season two games behind the Dodgers, Mays's conduct that day earned him the respect and admiration of the entire San Francisco sports community.

In 1966, Marichal (25–6) and Gaylord Perry (21–8) led the Giant pitching staff, while sluggers Mays, McCovey, and Jim Ray Hart combined to hit 106 home runs and drive in 292 runs. Along the way, Mays moved into second place behind Babe Ruth on the all-time home run list. He finished the year with a total of 542, but again the Giants fell short of the Dodgers.

The following year Mays's batting average dropped to .263—his lowest ever for a full season. This time the Giants finished 10½ games behind the St. Louis Cardinals.

Mays came back with a .289 average in 1968, but the Giants pitching staff was no match for Bob Gibson and the Cardinals. St. Louis got its second pennant in a row, while the Giants got their fourth straight runner-up finish, 9 games off the pace. Herman Franks was relieved of his duties as manager with Clyde King set to take over the next season.

There were even bigger changes to come in 1969, when the Montreal Expos and San Diego Padres joined the National League. The now 12–team league split into two divisions, East and West. The winner of each would meet in a post-season championship series to determine the pennant winner.

A knee injury limited Mays to only 117 games that season, and his totals dropped sharply to 13 home runs and 58 RBI's. To make matters worse, a rift between Mays and King developed over playing time and widened as the year progressed.

The high point of Mays's season came on September 22nd, when he hit the 600th home run of his career. Still, as the 1969 season ended with the Giants in second place for a record fifth straight time (3 games behind the Atlanta Braves), people were beginning to wonder aloud whether it was time for the 39–year-old legend to hang up his cleats.

But Mays wasn't ready to quit yet. In their 12 seasons in California, he and the Giants had compiled the best overall record of any National League team. And all they had to show for it was one pennant (1962).

Willie Mays wanted another shot at a World Series.

8

BACK TO WHERE IT ALL BEGAN

In 1970 the Giants got off to their worst start since moving to San Francisco. The team had a losing 19–25 record when manager Clyde King was replaced by Charlie Fox in mid-season. Almost immediately, the team improved, finishing behind Cincinnati and Los Angeles at a .531 pace.

Mays, meanwhile, became the ninth player in major-league history to accumulate 3,000 hits, and the feat seemed to rejuvenate him. He went on to have his best overall season since 1966, batting .291 with 28 homers, 94 runs scored, and 83 RBI's.

Back in 1971 for his twentieth big-league season, Mays started the year with a bang. He hit home runs in each of the Giants' first four games! Although he could not continue at that pace, he posted numbers that would make any 40-year-old proud. Pitchers still feared him, as his career-high, league-leading 112 bases on balls clearly showed. And by getting on base so often, he was able to steal 23 bases, his best haul since 1960.

Inspired by their leader, the Giants jumped out to an early lead in the National League West

Mays gets his 600th home run while pinch hitting against the San Diego Padres on September 22, 1969. Here, Coach Ozzie Virgil congratulates him as he rounds third.

race and finished first in their division. Then they moved on to play the East's top team, the Pittsburgh Pirates, in a best-of-five championship series for the N.L. pennant.

The Giants won the opener in San Francisco. But despite Mays's two-run homer in the second game, Pittsburgh won the playoff, 3 games to 1. Once again Mays and the Giants fell short of their ultimate goal—another World Series appearance.

During the off-season, Mays married Mae Louise Allen, and the two looked forward to their life together. But one thing they hadn't planned on occurred early in the 1972 season. On May 11th, Mays was traded to the New York Mets in exchange for pitcher Charlie Williams and $50,000.

After the initial shock wore off, Mays's reaction was positive. "When you come back to New York," he said, "it's like coming back to paradise."

Mays's first game in a Met uniform seemed straight out of a Hollywood movie. He came to bat with the score tied 4–all and hit a game-winning home run. New York's opponent? None other than the San Francisco Giants.

Mays averaged only .250 for the season, however, with 8 home runs in just 88 games. Still, the Mets finished third in the N.L. East while the Giants limped home fifth in the West.

Mays's career had been remarkably free of injuries, but age was beginning to take its toll. In July of 1973, he decided to finish out the season and then retire. After being informed of his decision, the Mets announced plans to hold Willie Mays Night on September 25th.

Nearly 55,000 fans jammed Shea Stadium on that special night. But before his long career finally ended, there would be one final moment of glory for Willie Mays. With the Mets involved in a pennant race, owner Joan Payson convinced Mays

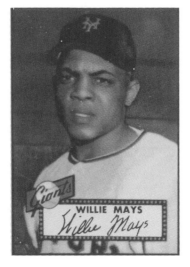

*Mays's 1952 Topps
bubblegum card*

to remain with the team through the stretch run. Despite a record just barely over .500, the Mets managed to win the 1973 National League East title in the closest divisional race ever. They moved on to play Cincinnati for the league championship and shocked the Reds by winning the best-of-five series, 3 games to 2.

The Mets—and Mays—were going to Oakland to play the A's in the World Series!

After losing the opener 2–1, the Mets were leading 6–4 in game 2 as the A's came to bat in the 9th inning. Mays was moved into center field for defensive purposes and, ironically, misplayed a ball which helped Oakland rally to tie the score.

Batting in the 12th inning, however, Mays had a chance to redeem himself. With two runners on base, he stepped to the plate to face Oakland's star reliever, Rollie Fingers. Always thinking, Mays turned to catcher Ray Fosse and said, "Gee, you know, Ray, it's tough to see the ball with that background. I hope he doesn't throw me any fastballs. I don't want to get hurt."

Sure enough, Fingers threw a fastball. Mays walloped it through the middle to drive in the game-winning run. The Series was tied at one game apiece.

The Mets won two of the three games in New York, but dropped the final two in Oakland, and the A's became world champions. Mays ended his magnificent career by getting 2 hits in 7 World Series at-bats for a .286 average.

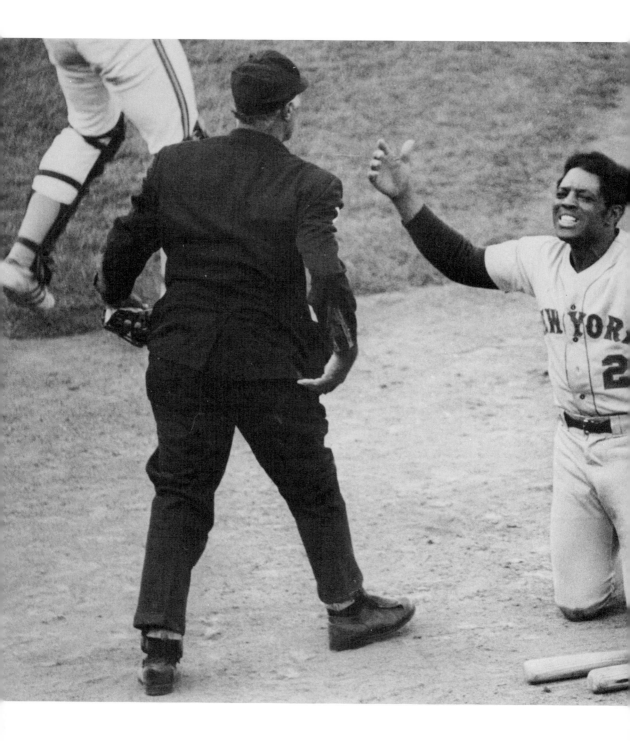

9

AMONG THE IMMORTALS

Even after his retirement, honors continued to come Mays's way, as he continued on with the Mets in an advisory capacity. But the greatest honor of all did not come until five years after his final appearance on a baseball field, when he was elected to the Baseball Hall of Fame in Cooperstown, New York.

When the ballots from the Baseball Writers' Association of America were counted, Mays's name was on 94.6 percent of them. That was the highest percentage of votes received by any player since the first year of voting, when Ty Cobb (98.2 percent), Babe Ruth (95.1 percent), and Honus Wagner (95.1 percent) were elected to the Hall.

An emotional Mays summed up his feelings about the national pastime in his speech at the induction ceremonies in 1979:

"What can I say? This country is made up of a great many things. You can grow up to be what

Mays' appeal to umpire Augie Donetelli was in vain. The Mets lost the 1973 World Series to Oakland in 7 games.

Traded to the New York Mets, Mays is interviewed at Shea Stadium.

you want. I chose baseball, and I loved every minute of it. I give you one word—love. It means dedication. You have to sacrifice many things to play baseball. I sacrificed a bad marriage and I sacrificed a good marriage. But I'm here today because baseball is my number-one love."

Shortly after his induction, Mays's association with baseball came to an unexpected halt. He had been offered a lucrative position with the new Bally's casino in Atlantic City. Although the job required little more than playing golf in a promotional capacity, baseball commissioner Bowie Kuhn told him he could not remain in baseball as long as he was connected with gambling in any way. Mays left his job with the Mets and became an outcast in the eyes of the game he loved. A similar fate befell fellow Hall of Famer Mickey Mantle, who would later suffer the same punishment at Kuhn's hands. The unhappy incident eventually worked itself out, however.

In 1985, Peter Ueberroth became baseball's

new commissioner. Obviously in disagreement with Kuhn's decision, Ueberroth did not see anything wrong with Mays's job. He announced that Mays and Mantle would both be allowed back in the game. "I am bringing back two players who are more a part of baseball than perhaps anyone else," he said.

Mays has since been employed by the San Francisco Giants. His official title is Special Assistant to the President and General Manager. He serves the club in a community relations and public relations capacity, and attends spring training with the team in Arizona. There, he spends time working with the outfielders. One of the players who has benefited from his help is Kevin Mitchell, the National League's Most Valuable Player for 1989.

To list Willie Mays's other accomplishments would take several pages. The following are just a few that can be added to those already mentioned. In 21 full seasons, he won 11 Gold Glove awards for fielding excellence and made it into the all-time top ten in the following categories: games (6th), at-bats (6th), runs scored (5th), hits (9th), home runs (3rd), total bases (3rd), runs batted in (7th), slugging average (10th), extra base hits (4th), and putouts by an outfielder (1st).

But all these numbers can hardly sum up Willie Mays the ballplayer. Leo Durocher came a lot closer with a few simple words. "Willie Mays," the former Giant manager said, "is the greatest player I ever laid eyes on!"

CHRONOLOGY

May 6, 1931	Willie Howard Mays is born in Westfield, Alabama
1948–49	Plays Negro League ball with the Birmingham Black Barons
1950	Signs his first pro contract with the New York Giants for $4,000 bonus
May 25, 1951	Makes big-league debut against the Philadelphia Phillies
May 28, 1951	Gets his first major-league hit—a home run—off Warren Spahn of the Braves
Oct. 3, 1951	Giants win pennant by defeating Dodgers in final game of the playoffs
Nov. 15, 1951	Mays named N.L. Rookie of the Year
May 29, 1952	Inducted into military service
March 1, 1954	Rejoins Giants following his Army discharge
Oct. 2, 1954	Giants defeat Indians in World Series
Dec. 16, 1954	Mays is named National League's Most Valuable Player; wins batting title with .345 average
1955	Leads N.L. in home runs (51)
Feb. 14, 1956	Marries Marghuerite Wendell
Aug. 19, 1957	Giants announce plans to move to California in 1958
Apr. 30, 1961	Mays hits 4 home runs against the Braves
Oct. 3, 1962	Giants win pennant by defeating the Dodgers in final game of the playoffs
1963	Mays and wife are divorced
1963	Mays signs $105,000 contract to become highest-paid player in history
May, 1964	Named team captain of Giants
1965	Named National League's Most Valuable Player; leads league in home runs (52) for fourth time
Sept. 22, 1969	Hits 600th career home run
1969	Named to "Baseball's Greatest Living Players" team
Jan. 17, 1970	Named *The Sporting News's* Player of the Decade for the 1960s
July 18, 1970	Gets 3,000th big-league hit
1971	Marries Mae Louise Allen
May 11, 1972	Is traded to New York Mets in exchange for pitcher Charlie Williams and $50,000
March, 1974	Inducted into Black Athletes Hall of Fame
1978	Named baseball's All-Time All-Star
1979	Inducted into major-league baseball's Hall of Fame

WILLIE HOWARD MAYS, Jr.
"THE SAY HEY KID"
NEW YORK N.L., SAN FRANCISCO N.L.,
NEW YORK N.L., 1951-1973
ONE OF BASEBALL'S MOST COLORFUL AND
EXCITING STARS. EXCELLED IN ALL PHASES OF
THE GAME. THIRD IN HOMERS (660), RUNS (2,062)
AND TOTAL BASES (6,066); SEVENTH IN HITS
(3,283) AND RBI'S (1,903). FIRST IN PUTOUTS
BY OUTFIELDER (7,095). FIRST TO TOP BOTH
300 HOMERS AND 300 STEALS. LED LEAGUE IN
BATTING ONCE, SLUGGING FIVE TIMES, HOME
RUNS AND STEALS FOUR SEASONS. VOTED N.L.
MVP IN 1954 AND 1965. PLAYED IN 24
ALL-STAR GAMES - A RECORD.

MAJOR LEAGUE STATISTICS

NEW YORK GIANTS, SAN FRANCISCO GIANTS, NEW YORK METS

Year	TEAM	G	AB	R	H	2B	3B	HR	RBI	BA	SB
1951	NY N	121	464	59	127	22	5	20	68	.274	7
1952		34	127	17	30	2	4	4	23	.236	4
1953		In military service									
1954		151	564	119	195	33	13	41	110	.345	8
1955		152	580	123	185	18	13	51	127	.319	24
1956		152	578	101	171	27	8	36	84	.296	40
1957		152	585	112	195	26	20	35	97	.333	38
1958	SF N	152	600	121	208	33	11	29	96	.347	31
1959		151	575	125	180	43	5	34	104	.313	27
1960		153	595	107	190	29	12	29	103	.319	25
1961		154	572	129	176	32	3	40	123	.308	18
1962		162	621	130	189	36	5	49	141	.304	18
1963		157	596	115	187	32	7	38	103	.288	5
1964		157	578	121	171	21	9	47	111	.296	19
1965		157	558	118	177	21	3	52	112	.317	9
1966		152	552	99	159	29	4	37	103	.288	5
1967		141	486	83	128	22	2	22	70	.263	6
1968		148	498	84	144	20	5	23	79	.289	12
1969		117	403	64	114	17	3	13	58	.283	6
1970		139	478	94	139	15	2	28	83	.291	5
1971		136	417	82	113	24	5	18	61	.271	23
1972	2 teams	SF N (19 G — .184)			NY N (69 G — .267)						
	total	88	244	35	61	11	1	8	22	.250	4
1973		66	209	24	44	10	0	6	25	.211	1
Totals		2,992	10,881	2,062	3,283	523	140	660	1,903	.302	338
World Series (4 years)		20	71	9	17	3	0	0	6	.239	2
All-Star Games (20 years)		24	75	20	23	2	3	3	9	.307	6

FURTHER READING

Chieger, Bob. *Voices of Baseball—Quotations on the Summer Game.* New York: New American Library, 1984.

Einstein, Charles. *A Flag for San Francisco.* New York: Simon & Schuster, 1962.

Einstein, Charles. *Willie's Time.* New York: J. B. Lippincott Company, 1979.

Getz, Mike. *Baseball's 3000–Hit Men.* Brooklyn, NY: Gemmeg Press, 1982.

Hodges, Russ, and Al Hirshberg. *My Giants.* Garden City, NY: Doubleday & Co., 1963.

Karst, Gene, and Martin J.Jones, Jr. *Who's Who in Professional Baseball.* New Rochelle, NY: Arlington House, 1973.

King, Joe. *The San Francisco Giants.* Englewood Cliffs, NJ: Prentice-Hall, 1958.

Klink, Bill. "Willie's Wonder Year." *Sports History.* March 1989, pp.48–49.

Mays, Willie, with Lou Sahadi. *Say Hey: The Autobiography of WIllie Mays.* New York: Simon & Schuster, 1988.

Reidenbaugh, Lowell. *The Sporting News Selects Baseball's 25 Greatest Pennant Races.* St. Louis MO: The Sporting News Publishing Co., 1987.

Stein, Fred, and Nick Peters. *Giants Diary.* Berkeley, CA: North Atlantic Books, 1987.

Stein, Fred. *Under Coogan's Bluff.* New York: Fred Stein, 1978.

Sugar, Bert Randolph. *Baseball's 50 Greatest Games.* New York: Exeter Books, 1986.

INDEX

llen, Mae Louise, 52
lou, Felipe, 39
lou, Matty, 43
malfitano, Joey, 37
ntonelli, Johnny, 29
unt Sarah, 26
ailey, Ed, 39
oston Braves, 10, 15
owman 1951 bubble gum card, 52
ranca, Ralph, 22
rooklyn Dodgers, 15, 21, 26, 31, 32
andlestick Park, 36
epeda, Orlando, 35, 39
incinatti Reds, 37, 51, 53
obb, Ty, 40, 55
ark, Alvin, 33, 36, 40, 46
avis, Piper, 13
iMaggio, Joe, 34
oby, Larry, 27, 28
odger-Giant rivalry, 21, 22, 39, 41, 48
urocher, Leo, 18, 19, 23, 26, 28, 29,
   31, 32, 57
airfield, Alabama, 14
arrell, Dick, 41
eller, Bob ,28
ingers, Rollie, 53
ort Eustis, 25, 26
ox, Charlie, 51
oxx, Jimmie, 47
ranks, Herman, 47, 49
arcia, Mike, 27
enovese, Chick, 15, 16
ibson, Bob, 49
iles, Warren, 48
oosby, David and Anna, 20
all of Fame, 55
art, Jim Ray, 48
earn, Jim, 21
omestead Greys, 15
vin, Monte, 20, 21, 29, 36
ansen, Larry, 36
ing, Clyde, 49, 51
oufax, Sandy, 39, 40, 48
uhn, Bowie, 56
abine, Clem, 21
ane, Frank, 33
emon, Bob, 27
iddle, Don, 28

Lockman, Whitey, 36
Los Angeles Dodgers, 35, 39, 40, 41,
   42, 48, 51
Maglie, Sal, 27
Mantle, Mickey, 56
Marichal, Juan, 48
Mays, Michael, 38, 45
Mays, Willie
   All-Star game, 26
   bankruptcy, 45
   "basket" catch, 25, 26
   batting title, 27
   divorce, 45
   drafted in the Army, 24, 25
   elected Hall of Fame, 55, 60
   fatigue, 34, 40, 46
   500th home run, 47
   first Major League game, 9
   Gold Glove awards, 57
   Harlem, 20
   home-run title, 47
   in minor leagues, 15, 16, 17
   list of accomplishments, 56
   marriage, 32, 52
   NL Most Valuable Player (MVP),
      29, 44, 47
   parents, 13
   Rookie of the Year, 23
   600th home run, 49, 50
   3,000th hit, 51
   traded to Mets, 52
Milwaukee Braves, 35, 36
Minneapolis Millers, 12, 16, 17
Minneapolis Tribune, 16, 17
"Miracle at Coogan's Bluff," 21
Mize, Johnny, 31
McCovey, Willie, 37, 39. 43, 48
Montague, Eddie, 15
Montreal Expos, 49
Negro League World Series, 15
Newcombe, Don, 22
New York City, 27, 52
New York Giants, 9, 12, 15, 19, 21, 25,
   29, 31, 32, 34
New York Mets, 45, 52, 53, 54
New York Yankees, 21, 23, 34, 42, 43
Oakland Athletics, 53
Oliver, Gene, 41

Ott, Mel, 47
Payson, Joan, 52
Perry, Gaylord, 48
Perry, Alonzo, 15
Philadelphia Phillies, 9
Pierce, Billy, 41, 42
Pittsburgh Pirates, 32, 40, 52
Podres, Johnny, 39
Polo Grounds, 10, 20, 21, 27, 28, 33,
   45, 46
Rhodes, Dusty, 29
Rickwood Field, 14
Rigney, Bill, 32, 34, 36
Roebuck, Ed, 39, 42
Roseboro, John, 47
Ruth, Babe, 47, 48,
St. Louis Cardinals, 10, 11, 33, 41, 49
San Diego Padres, 49, 50
Sanford, Jack, 43
San Francisco Chronicle, 35
San Francisco fans, 34, 35, 43, 45
San Francisco Giants, 34, 39, 52
San Francisco Giants opening day
   lineup, 37
Seals Stadium, 36
Shea, Bill, 46
Shea Stadium, 52, 56
Sheehan, Tom, 36
Sherry, Larry, 39
Spahn, Warren 11, 19
Stanky, Eddie, 20
Stoneham, Horace, 17, 31, 36, 46
"The Shot Heard 'Round the World," 22
"The Catch", 28, 29
Thompson, Hank, 29
Thomson, Bobby, 21, 22
Ueberroth, Peter, 56
Wendell Marghuerite, 32, 45
Wertz, Vic, 28
Westfield, Alabama, 13
Westrum, Wes, 36
Williams, Charlie, 52
Williams, Ted, 26, 47
Wills, Maury, 39
Willie Mays Night, 46, 52
World Series, 22, 27, 28, 29, 42, 54,
   53
Wynn, Early, 27, 29

PICTURE CREDITS
Birmingham Public Library, Birmingham, AL: p.14; National Archives, Washington, DC: pp. 33, 37, 58; National Baseball Library,
Cooperstown, NY: p. 60; San Francisco Giants: pp. 44, 47; reprinted with permission of the Star Tribune, Minneapolis-St.Paul, MN:
p.16; copyright The Topps Company, Inc.: p. 52; UPI/Bettmann: pp. 2, 8, 10, 12, 18, 20, 22, 24, 28, 30, 35, 38, 40, 42, 50, 54, 56

JOHN F. GRABOWSKI was educated at the City College of New York, where he was a member of the baseball team, and at Teachers College, Columbia University, where he received his master's in educational psychology. He currently teaches high school math and computer studies on Staten Island. He is a free-lance writer who has had several hundred pieces published in newspapers, magazines, and the programs of professional teams. The author of *Super Sports Word Find Puzzles*, *Dodgers Trivia*, *Cleveland Browns Trivia*, *San Francisco 49ers Trivia*, and *Detroit Tigers Trivia*, he published the monthly *Baseball Trivia Newsletter*. A nationally syndicated columnist, his weekly "Stat Sheet" is supplied to more than 600 newspapers.

JIM MURRAY, veteran sports columnist of the *Los Angeles Times*, is one of America's most acclaimed writers. He has been named "America's Best Sportswriter" by the National Association of Sportscasters and Sportswriters 14 times, was awarded the Red Smith Award, and was twice winner of the National Headliner Award. In addition, he was awarded the J. G. Taylor Spink Award in 1987 for "meritorious contributions to baseball writing." With this award came his 1988 induction into the National Baseball Hall of Fame in Cooperstown, New York.

EARL WEAVER is the winningest manager in Baltimore Orioles history by a wide margin. He compiled 1,480 victories in his 17 years at the helm. After managing eight different minor league teams, he was given the chance to lead the Orioles in 1968. Under his leadership the Orioles finished lower than second place in the American League East only four times in 17 years. One of only 12 managers in big league history to have managed in four or more World Series, Earl was named Manager of the Year in 1979. The popular Weaver had his number 5 retired in 1982, joining Brooks Robinson, Frank Robinson, and Jim Palmer, whose numbers were retired previously. Earl Weaver continues his association with the professional baseball scene by writing, broadcasting, and coaching.